Looking through Jesus

Alan Bartlett

Lenten reflections on St Luke's Gospel

kevin mayhew

kevin
mayhew

First published in Great Britain in 2017 by Kevin Mayhew Ltd
Buxhall, Stowmarket, Suffolk IP14 3BW
Tel: +44 (0) 1449 737978 Fax: +44 (0) 1449 737834
E-mail: info@kevinmayhew.com

www.kevinmayhew.com

9 8 7 6 5 4 3 2 1 0

ISBN 978 1 84867 930 6
Catalogue No. 1501564

Cover design by Rob Mortonson
© Image used under licence from Shutterstock Inc.
Edited by Virginia Rounding
Typeset by Angela Selfe

Printed and bound in Great Britain

Contents

About the author

Alan has been vicar of three churches around Durham City for nine years and is moving to become Clergy Development Advisor for Durham Diocese. Previously he was in charge of the post-graduate degrees at Cranmer Hall and taught spirituality, church history, practical theology and Anglicanism. He is still involved in theological education. He has degrees from the universities of Cambridge, Birmingham and Durham and has served in the North East since 1991.

His Bible Studies have already been widely published. He is the author of *Humane Christianity, A Passionate Balance* and contributed to *The Christian Handbook of Abuse, Addiction and Difficult Behaviour* and *Faith Matters – A Comprehensive Introduction to Christianity and Christian Faith*, both published by Kevin Mayhew.

Before ordination Alan was a youth worker, housing worker and research student. Alan is married to Helen, a Railway Chaplain, and they have two adult children and two dogs, Bennie and Pip.

Introduction

Many of us know what we are supposed to think about Jesus. He is God's Son. The Incarnate One. God in human form. God with a human face. The image of the invisible God (Colossians 1:15). The Word of God from before the creation of the universe (John 1:1). In short, Jesus is God (John 20:28).

But we also know that Jesus of Nazareth was a real flesh-and-blood human being. He clearly got tired, even irritable, hungry, thirsty and frightened, and he died a terrible death after ruthless torture and public humiliation. All too human. And it is also true – if we can bring ourselves to admit it – that whilst some of the time his words and actions are sublime, the most truthful words ever spoken and actions of lump-in-the-throat compassion, all of which we would expect of God in human form, at other times his words and actions are baffling, hard, or even off-putting.

We say in the creeds, Jesus was both truly God and truly human. It took the Church several hundred years to reach this apparently simple form of words, which even at the time was not understood by all, and has remained the source of deep exploration and some controversy ever since. But it is the theological and spiritual discipline within which the Church has placed itself and within which, as an English Anglican vicar, I am placed. I am happy to be located here.

But I worry, as we read little sections of the story of Jesus, Sunday by Sunday in our Eucharists, Masses, Communion services and elsewhere, that Jesus remains a bit baffling, and so remains distant. He is either floating a foot above the ground, beyond contradiction, scarcely human, more like a divine superman, or he is a wandering Jewish rabbi in a complex and contested ancient world, and it takes a lot of work to get from then and there to here and now, let alone to God in human form.

So we end up with some odd ideas about God or we retain images of a distant God to whom Jesus bears an uncertain relation. Either way, Jesus does not really bring us closer to God. And we are more comfortable talking about 'God' than about 'Jesus'. So we emaciate our distinctive Christian faith.

And all this of course in a world where, even if we don't often say it out loud in church, it is increasingly hard to feel that Jesus is *the* way to God. Surely there are other routes to God? And indeed, isn't it true that 'if it works for you' (whatever that quite means), then 'each to his or her own'? Inside, we feel we can't really claim too much for Jesus, whatever our songs, services and scriptures say. So we end up with an internal disconnect which has the effect of reinforcing our bafflement at Gospel readings and sermons and so our sense of puzzlement with Jesus and distance from God.

This is quite a big agenda and this little book of thoughts and longings and reflections is not going to address it all! But I have had a sense for a while that, if we really spend time with the Jesus presented to us in the Gospels – honest, slow time – then we might or might not be able to resolve some of the puzzles but, above all, we will meet him again. And in meeting him, experience that deep humanity which we still find so attractive, and move through that to see God in him. And so meet God in him. But that is the order of working. Look slowly and honestly first. Get the humanity. Let the divinity come through to us. Because I believe it will, and that will be life-giving.[1] [2]

A couple more words about the book. We are going to be looking at just one Gospel, that of Luke. We are doing this for two reasons. First, while it is clear that there are intricate and still unresolved connections between the four Gospels, our habit of mixing them all together to produce one 'coherent' story has had the odd result that we hear each of the Gospels less clearly. The newer lectionaries, when we spend time each year with (mostly) one of the Gospels, are helping to rebalance this. But our instinct, for good reasons, is often to try to put 'the original story' together and that

---

1. As is clear from the opening sentences of this book, this is not an original way of thinking about Jesus and God. Indeed, I suspect that my feelings about this come from a previous generation of often Anglican writers about Jesus and God whom I encountered during my ministerial training. John A.T. Robinson, *The Human Face of God* (London: SCM, 1972). John V. Taylor, *The Christlike God* (London: SCM, 1992). Both of these look back to Michael Ramsey and his wonderful statement: 'God is Christlike and in him is no un-Christlikeness at all.' A.M. Ramsey, *God, Christ and the World* (London: SCM, 1969), p.98. My little book is operating at a much less sophisticated level than these, and I would not want to follow them in all their conclusions. In some ways, the titles are what have most inspired me.
2. I am not trying to make any technical Christological or Trinitarian points in this discussion. But careful readers will notice a deliberate ambiguity: Jesus both points us to God beyond himself and embodies God in himself.

can stop us seeing what is before our eyes in the words of a Gospel. And whilst it is surely right not to spend so much time on Luke's theology that we don't get through that to meet Jesus and God – that would be a mockery of everything Luke was trying to do – yet the way Luke tells this story is through his own ears and eyes and heart and mind and spirit. It is unique to Luke. So we will try to see Jesus, and God, with and through Luke.

Now at this point I must add that this is not quite how Luke himself works. The divinity of Jesus is not hidden in Luke, as it is in Mark. From early on in his Gospel, Luke makes it clear that Jesus is the Son of God and clear flashes of divinity are present in the Nativity Story, for example, as well as throughout the Gospel. (Let's shelve the question of what 'divinity' might look like for a moment, but one thing I think Luke means by it is divine power and having re-read my own book, I realise that is what I think too!) It is also true that, as in Mark, we also see a very human Jesus in Luke. Indeed, in some ways, the portrayal of Jesus in Luke is for many Christians the most sympathetic and accessible. So in reading Luke from humanity to divinity, or rather seeing the divinity in the humanity,[3] we are both going with

---

3. There could be here a technical discussion of Luke's Christology and Trinitarianism... But I simply want to note my indebtedness to some penetrating questions from my colleague, Richard Briggs, about the nature of New Testament Christology, the current debates in this area and pointing me to further reading. I was especially struck by R. Bauckham's *God Crucified* (Carlisle: Paternoster, 1998). He wrote: 'while the Fathers successfully appropriated, in their own way in Nicene theology, the New Testament's inclusion of Jesus in the identity of God, they were less successful in appropriating this corollary, the revelation of the divine identity in Jesus' human life and passion'. (p.ix) This was my experience too in reading the historical commentaries on Luke. I think modern sensibilities help us to see the radicalism of Jesus in Luke more clearly. And that takes us to a more radical God.

the grain of Luke's Gospel, (Luke surely wanted us to be attracted by his account of Jesus of Nazareth), as well as reading it in a way against the deep shape of the Gospel. There will be places where I will find myself saying, 'this is what Luke says, and perhaps why, and doesn't it make good sense?' while in other places I will say, 'this is what Luke says, and perhaps why, but I find myself thinking and feeling something else because of the world *I* live in'. It is crucial to be honest in biblical study, and so I will be explicit when I am 'reading against the text' so that you as reader can make up your own mind, even whilst I am trying to persuade you. But again, all this is not a million miles from how Luke wrote for 'Theophilus'. Luke too was trying to persuade his hearers and readers to see God through Jesus.

There is a second reason for focusing on Luke. A simple practical reason: if I know anything about the Bible, it is about Luke. (Not that 'knowing' is the essential to meeting God through Luke, but it may help you as the reader to relax into the book if you think I have done at least a little background study!) This reflects my own preferences, because I think that in Luke we do see Jesus at his most humane and inclusive. And in our context – I write as vicar of a group of north-eastern Anglican churches – humanity and accessibility are crucial ways into Jesus and God. This is the third time I have had a go at reflecting in writing on Luke,[4] and I am not bored yet!

---

4. If a reader wants a flavour of slightly longer reflections set in a more explicit theological framework, then I recommend they read the extended Bible studies at the end of each chapter in A. Bartlett, *Humane Christianity* (London: DLT, 2004).

It is also worth saying that, whilst Jesus has always been an attractive figure for Christians, as I look at him from my location in the early twenty-first century in north-east England, I am struck by the contrast with how earlier generations saw him and that I am wanting to see him as a more radical, non-establishment, less conformist and certainly less authoritarian figure. I think there is depth and strength in how we see Jesus now. You as reader will have to make up your own mind whether this is a valid and a fair reading of Jesus in Luke.

I should say at this point that I have benefited hugely from working alongside professional biblical scholars. In particular, I am grateful to the Revd Professor Walter Moberly of the Department of Theology and Religion in Durham University who, a generation ago, helped me to realise that it was OK to ask honest questions about the Gospels without being either disbelieving or disloyal, and has continued to help me to read the Bible with 'full imaginative seriousness'.[5] It is also a huge privilege to have a former colleague from Cranmer Hall, St John's College, Durham (the Anglican theological college), the Revd Dr Richard Briggs, now working as our 'curate'. Richard is an amphibious biblical scholar (able to inhabit both academia and the Church) and has kindly dipped into this book and given invaluable feedback. Dr Melody Briggs, another expert on Luke

---

5. The original article which opened my eyes and my heart and spirit is not so accessible now, but see 'Proclaiming Christ Crucified: Some Reflections on the Use and Abuse of the Gospels', *Anvil* 5 (1988), 31-52.

and an experienced adult educator, also read and commented very helpfully. Any errors of course remain my responsibility.

And whilst I am saying thank you, I must thank John Cox (the Director of Ordinands who saw me through the discernment process a quarter of a century ago!) for inviting me to write this book and Virginia Rounding, editor, for improving it hugely; Adrian and Marian Greenwood for the kind use of their holiday home where some of this book was written; and also the Anglican Franciscan brothers in Alnmouth where the book was finished; and the people of St Giles', St Mary's and St Cuthbert's who, often unwittingly, have helped write this book too, as their baffled faces have looked back at me during one of my interminable sermons . . .

The book works by choosing mostly sequential readings from Luke. However, even with all this time to read it, we will not read every single verse in Luke. Sorry if I have missed out one of your favourite passages! The book was written to be read during Lent, so we mostly miss the Christmas and Resurrection stories, but the book does touch on Christmas when we reflect on Joseph and Mary, and it finishes with part of Luke's account of the Resurrection.

And, finally, I have put some recommendations for further reading at the back of the book. I do hope that you will carry on reading and thinking and studying. Above all, just after I had started writing this book, I found on a bookshelf this book by Anselm Grün: *Jesus:*

the Image of Humanity. Grün is a German Benedictine abbot, but we clearly share similar concerns and passions. He expresses so well what I am trying to do:

> Some people think that Luke was only a good storyteller, but not a good theologian. I can't share this view. Luke understands the art of telling the story of Jesus in such a way that the whole theology of the incarnation lights up. Jesus doesn't need to assert and explain that Jesus is the Son of God. He tells the story of Jesus in such a way that the divine shines out in Jesus. As readers are touched by Jesus, so God dawns on them, and in this way they are drawn into the event of the incarnation.

And as he says:

> I want every reader to be guided by Luke to Jesus, to gain new insights into Jesus and to discover in him the one who gives meaning to our existence, heals our wounds and leads us to true life.[6]

Amen.

---

6. A. Grün, *Jesus: the image of humanity* (First published 2001. English translation, London: Continuum, 2003), pp.3, 13.

1

(Ash Wednesday)
The parable of the Pharisee and the tax collector
Luke 18:9-14

Parables are stories that bite back! It is interesting that Jesus of Nazareth told stories and parables as his main way of helping people to ponder, rather than teaching concepts. So he got under people's skin and wanted them to do some of the work of thinking for themselves.

Jesus is faced by people who thought they were in the right, good enough for God and better than others. He told them this story.

We are conditioned to think of Pharisees as self-righteous by definition, but in Jesus' day they were the people trying to help everyone to be holy for God, so that the Messiah would come. But trying to help other people to be good is a dangerous occupation. And they did get a bit self-righteous ...

So the Pharisee has gone into the Temple (the equivalent of all our Christian cathedrals rolled into one) to pray. He spots the tax-collector out of the corner of his eye. His stomach turns. 'What is the tax-collector doing in this holy place? He is a thief, a collaborator, a bully. He is not fit to be here. Thank you, God, that I am not like him, or like any of those other *unrespectable* people.' And then, in case God has forgotten, the

Pharisee reminds God of how serious he is about faith – fasting twice a week and tithing his giving. (Actually, that is quite an impressive spiritual discipline . . .)

But as I read this, my own stomach turns. 'Lord, I thank you that I am not like this self-righteous Pharisee. I am not proud or hypocritical like him, or indeed like those other people over there . . .'

Snap. The jaws of the parable close on us. Because it suddenly makes us realise that we are being just as self-righteous as the Pharisee. Instead, we are invited to imitate the tax-collector who just said, 'God, forgive me.' Why did Jesus do this?

This is not grovelling to God. It is honesty about ourselves. If you are reading this on Ash Wednesday, it is what Lent is really about: self-examination. I think Jesus thought that if we were only more real about ourselves we would be able to be more real about and with God.

2
The birth of John the Baptist foretold
Luke 1:5-17

These are good people. A lovely older, devout, faithful, but childless couple. And then God blesses them with a son. All is happy. But we know that this promised boy will grow up to be John the Baptist, who will have a demanding and painful job to do.

John is to be pure – teetotal – and will be filled from birth with God's Spirit. He will be like the greatest of the Hebrew prophets. He will make peace in families and help the disobedient to become good and wise. So they are fit and ready to meet 'the Lord'. In plays and films, John the Baptist is almost always portrayed as a shouty man, dressed in animal clothes, hairy. Our image of a prophet. Scary.

So if the one who prepares the way is like this, how much more scary will be 'the Lord' when he comes?

But Jesus was not as scary as this, especially to sinners. It baffled John, as we shall see later. But why, if Jesus is coming to help people to be good, did he not frighten them into goodness, like John did? So how might God go about the task of making us good now?

3

The judgement on Zechariah
Luke 1:18-22

As if to add to the scariness of John the Baptist, when Zechariah doubts the angel (God) – for good reason, 'I am an old man, and my wife is getting on in years' – he is judged. He is made mute, unable to speak of what he has seen. Indeed it will all get very embarrassing. When John is born and about to be named, Zechariah still can't speak and has to write down John's name so the baby is dedicated correctly.

The Bible has many stories about God judging people, often with unpleasant consequences. At least Zechariah got his voice back. Look at what happened to Pharaoh! So whether we are comfortable reading this story as literally true or as a beautiful story written to make a point, we get it. Doubting an angel (God) brings punishment. So doubting is wrong and God punishes doubters . . .

So why is Jesus gentle with those who struggle to believe? As we will see, he rarely judges those who struggle to believe. Rather, he takes even the little crumb of faith which they have and works with it.

We have an odd relationship with the image of God judging. We may sometimes want God to judge others – dictators, crooks, abusers – but on the whole we do not want be judged ourselves. Or think we deserve to be judged. Except in the dark recesses of our minds, when the scary God of judgement is our nightmare . . . perhaps God really is the judge?

Luke seems to have inherited quite a traditional image of the God of judgement. And as we shall see later in his Gospel, at times he writes about Jesus in such a way as to make sure that Jesus' judgement is made visible. Jesus of Nazareth was no softy. But I can't help but feel that, as Luke is writing this part of his Gospel, so he is setting up our nightmares about God, only to subvert them with the example of Jesus.

Which is the better image of God? The One who makes doubters mute, or the One who lets a prostitute touch him?

4
The judgement of John
Luke 3:1-9

Priests are supposed to be nice to people now. We have a bad record of being nasty to people and, anyway, we need everyone we can to come to church . . . So I would not be likely to start a sermon with 'you brood of vipers!'.

But that is just the first of the puzzles in this passage. These folk must have been deeply perplexed. Were they not doing exactly what John had asked for, to come and listen to him and be open to change? Especially as the change involved not just a change in how they lived, but being publicly washed (baptised) which was normally a rite kept for dirty Gentiles. And these are all the children of Abraham, so why do they need to be washed anyway?

Above all, it feels as if John was expecting people to make themselves be good enough to meet 'the Lord'. God's way, in the prophecy from Isaiah (40:3-5), seemed to involve everything being made perfect for God before God arrives; a bit like the Queen is reputed to live with the smell of fresh paint everywhere she visits!

Did Jesus do this? Did he expect people to be good enough to meet him? We shall see later in the book, but even at this stage, I guess we would say not.

Does God expect us to be good before we get to meet him? I sometimes think that, along with the unbelief and the indifference, there is also a sense in our society that 'I have to be good enough before I can meet God, or even just go to church with his people.' Is this what you really believe – buried deep in your psyche – that you are not good enough for God? We'll see how Jesus compares.

5

The Benedictus: a song of liberation?
Luke 1:67-79

Depending on how you are reading this little book, today
may be a Sunday. If you are a very traditional member
of the Church of England, you may already have been
to church and sung this canticle, the *Benedictus*. As a
choirboy I sang this every Sunday, during Mattins (from
the *Book of Common Prayer*), which was still then a main
Sunday service. This memory makes me feel very old
and brings home to me how much the Church has
changed in my own lifetime.

When the Church has changed so much so quickly,
it can be hard for us to keep our bearings. What are
we really here for? What is the Church for? Beautiful
worship as a gateway to God and a sort of gentle
community glue are my memories of those days. And I
am deeply grateful for them. They laid the foundations
of my own spiritual life. But I am not surprised that we
don't sing Mattins every Sunday any more. It was a bit
dry even then! So what are we to do now?

I suspect that Luke was conscious of living through a
spiritual revolution, one which perhaps to his amazement
would eventually turn the Roman Empire upside down.
So he wanted to help his readers make sense of what
was going on. And this canticle, sacred song, written to

sound like the Old Testament, was one way in which he did this. It resonated with so many of the promises in the Hebrew Bible about God rescuing his people. We know that some of Jesus' disciples took this sort of language literally – that Jesus would drive away the Romans – but Luke knew that was not what God was doing in Jesus. God was still about liberation but it went beyond life here and now, to life with God for ever. The *Benedictus* is poetry, which is partly why we still say and sing it, and as an English Anglican priest I do that most mornings in Morning Prayer. I almost always hear and feel something new in it about liberation by God.

But the sting in the tail is that much of the *Benedictus* is about John the Baptist's role in God's liberation. Zechariah's son has a huge job to do. How are we caught up in God's work of liberation now?

6

Jesus' Baptism
Luke 3:21, 22

Why was Jesus baptised? All the Gospels tell us he was baptised but none really explain why. Jesus wasn't seen as a sinner. He certainly wasn't a Gentile convert. John did not want to baptise him. So why did Jesus insist? Some guesses are better than others. That this was the moment when he offered himself and was commissioned for his public ministry. That it was an act of identification with his fellow human beings. Luke does not even begin to try to explain it.

Like all the Gospels, Luke's is shot through with 'miracle'. Each of the Gospel accounts of Jesus' baptism has a 'supernatural' element. Luke simply assumes it. Heaven is opened and the Holy Spirit comes down on Jesus in bodily form ('concrete' is one clunky comic modern translation). And then there is the voice from heaven. All very straightforward. But of course it isn't. And it wasn't even in Luke's day. We don't (often) hear audible voices from heaven and never actually see the Spirit as a physical dove. Luke may have different ways of telling the truth. Luke may even be more subtle in the genre of writing he uses. (We tend to jump between 'literal historical fact' and 'made-up story' with not much in between and all the time really feeling that only the former is really true. But think about the truth we learn in a great play or a good film or 'even' a deep fairy story.

And sometimes we know that what we are hearing is grown around a kernel of fact but has then been interpreted, and as with Luke, interpreted not by an academic explanation but by imagery.) But Luke clearly thinks this incident is very important, as do the other Gospel writers. Why?

Because in this story Jesus hears the voice from heaven affirming him: 'You are my Son.'

We know there was public gossip about Jesus' birth. Whilst the Greeks or Romans might have told stories about gods impregnating human women, the Jews did not. The Early Church was embarrassed about the story of the virgin birth (or rather virginal conception). And Jesus was referred to several times as 'Mary's son'. Not Joseph's son. Odd. Especially in that time and place. Something dodgy had happened.

So perhaps Jesus needed to hear this affirmation: 'You are my beloved Son. I am well pleased with you.' Perhaps he needed to hear it now, as he prepared to begin his public life and work?

How does thinking like that make you feel? It often feels a little impertinent – let alone difficult – to try to get into the mind of Jesus. But do we imagine Jesus not feeling worried or insecure? Did he always float six inches above the earth because of course, really, he is God? That's not how he appears in Luke and one thing we can be sure of is that this was a real flesh-and-blood human being who ate, walked, sailed, got hungry and thirsty and tired, and slept. And got frustrated and sad. Just like us. Just like any other human being. Heavenly voices did not take away the dirt beneath his toe nails. Jesus is one of us.

7

Jesus is tempted
Luke 4:1-13

This is yet another style of writing. How did Luke know any of this? Had Jesus told some of the disciples privately and they had passed it on to Luke (and to Matthew and a tiny bit to Mark)? But the story has the ring of truth.

When I was studying 'A' level history at school, we had a very fine, if slightly terrifying, history teacher, Mr 'Dan' Sturdey. Several of us went on to become professional historians in part because of his example and teaching. But he was frightening. One of those teachers you didn't mess about because of his innate authority. He was also prone to asking hard questions . . . Now this may be my youthful prejudices, but my memory is that Mr Sturdey was not a practising Christian, at all. One day – we must have been studying some power-mad despot – he asked: 'Who is the only person who was never corrupted by power?' It seemed like quite a sweeping question. And then he began to look at me. (I was known to be a keen Christian.) I could hear my brain saying, 'Jesus', but I can remember thinking: 'Don't say that. You'll just be mocked. Dan would not mean Jesus.' So I stayed silent until, in exasperation, Mr Sturdey said: 'Well, Jesus, of course.' And proceeded to read us the temptation story. We got it.

There are two ways of reading this story. That Jesus overcame temptation. Of course he did. He is God. Or that Jesus was really tempted, which is a bit puzzling if he is simply God.

I think these were real temptations for Jesus. To misuse his spiritual power. For his own gain. For glory. Even to convince others that what he said and did was true – a good temptation. But no, he won't perform miracles for his own benefit or to convince others. He keeps his integrity. And he will of course at the end let go of his power, but keep his integrity. Impressive and memorable. And unique. So what does this tell us about God?

8

Jesus explains his mission
Luke 4:14-21

We don't like big-heads (though given the growing culture of celebrity leadership in this country, we are losing our grip on this good old value). So is Jesus being big-headed here?

Jesus has come back to his home town. His fame has gone before him. We can imagine the hushed expectation in the synagogue as he stood up to read – and preach. Luke provides us with the briefest of summaries: 'Today this scripture has been fulfilled in your hearing.' Jesus is claiming for himself a 'messianic' role in bringing freedom, recovery, good news and blessing from God.

But it doesn't feel big-headed. It just feels right. This is partly because it is Jesus who does this. And it is partly because he does not do this with self-importance, but with the focus on those he is blessing.

And when we hear these words, it is always worth reminding ourselves again of what Jesus thought he was trying to do and what, therefore, we as his current disciples should be about. Blessing, liberating, enabling the flourishing of others. I don't think Jesus was very 'churchy'. But he did 'do God'. This is God's blessing that he is announcing and transmitting, to people who were really poor, ill and oppressed, not just looking like film extras in a movie.

Do we really believe that God wants people to flourish? How do we join in that mission? Here, now, where we live and worship?

9

Reaction
Luke 4:22-30

We like to think that goodness is always recognised and welcomed. It isn't. Perhaps Jesus has heard some muttering in the back row. He was never frightened to expose the mutterers. It can be hard to hear the truth from someone with whom we are familiar. After all, wasn't Jesus just Joseph's son, and wasn't Joseph just a carpenter? This is not a trained rabbi, let alone the Messiah. I wonder why they had been muttering, 'Doctor, heal yourself.' Did they think he was a bit mad in the head?

You can hear the unspoken mutterings. Surely God is predictable. He works with his own for his own. And so why did Jesus not start here in Nazareth? Amongst his own.

And Jesus goes straight for the jugular (I paraphrase): 'You don't trust me because you think you know me. But your God is too small and too narrow.' So he chooses two shocking examples of where God sent the most famous prophets to liberate those outside the official People of God. And it causes rage amongst the mutterers. Hatred. Enough to motivate attempted murder. We so often celebrate the 'Nazareth Manifesto', (which is the name the Church has given to this crucial summary by Jesus of his mission), without reading on to see how it was received.

I am writing this reflection on the day after the UK EU Referendum. By the time you read this, I have no idea what will be going on! But I am sure that someone somewhere will be saying: 'We can't look after them because they are not from round here. Get them out.'

Jesus directly challenges this way of feeling and thinking about God and other people. How does that make us feel?

10

Prayer
Luke 4:42-44

After the trouble in Nazareth, Jesus has moved on to Capernaum and is preaching in the synagogue again. Even in Luke's highly stylised account, we get some sense of the pressure on him. He is preaching and arguing in public again, challenging the local religious authorities. He is also confronting spiritual evil and bringing health and healing to the sick. Luke tells us that he laid his hands on every one of those who was sick (4:40). I suspect that may have been a bit gruesome as well as exhausting. His compassion seems endless.

But early in the morning, he goes out on his own to a deserted place, a 'lonely' place, presumably up in the hills, far away from villages and synagogues. Why? Luke doesn't tell us here, but we are told elsewhere that this was at least in part so he could pray.

I wonder what he was doing when he was praying? For much of his recorded life, Jesus seems to have had an intimate relationship with the God whom he called his 'abba', his Dad. So this feels like a time of renewing that intimate relationship. A perfect 'retreat'.

But notice what happens next. The people have come looking for him. Are there other sick to be healed?

Do they just love being with him? And certainly they don't want him to leave. But Jesus is restless, driven. He won't stay, even in this little town where he has been made so welcome and been so effective. He has been sent for other people too. So he strides off over the hills. His disciples talked of Jesus being consumed, burnt, by the love of God. I suspect that if we imagine Jesus' times of prayer with his heavenly Dad as being cosy and reassuring, we are getting it wrong. Jesus came away from 'retreat' with fire in his belly. Do we?

11

The calling of Peter
Luke 5:1-11

'You can tell a lot about a person by their friends!' So goes the old saying. Jesus had a very mixed group of friends. It certainly looks as if he brought together people who would not normally have spent time together, peacefully. Northerners and southerners. Pro- and anti-government. Educated and not educated. Those who worked with their hands and those who had soft hands.

Peter is a classic of one type. A fisherman. Certainly would have had rough hands and a weathered browned face. Probably smelt a bit fishy! And was in himself a bit impetuous, prone to sudden impulses and words.

Jesus is preaching. So many people have come to hear him – we shouldn't need to keep reminding ourselves that, for most of his life and with most ordinary people, Jesus was hugely popular, interesting – anyway, so many people have come to hear him that he needs a better platform from which to speak and so he borrows Peter's boat so he can speak over the water to the crowd.

When he is finished, Jesus wants to say, 'thank you'. A courteous man. So he suggests to Peter that they go fishing. Peter is perhaps less keen, thinking this is not a great 'thank-you' present. They had been fishing all night and caught nothing. Now either Jesus knew something about fishing, or got lucky, or Luke wants us to see his divine power at work – most likely – but they make a remarkable catch of fish.

Two thoughts. First: this is exactly the sort of Gospel story with which I struggle rationally. I too have been known to ask God to help me to find a car-parking space when pressed, but I know that this is not good theology . . . Jesus miraculously helping Peter and co. to catch fish is right on the end of what I can naturally believe. So I don't place great weight on this but it is worth us saying to each other that, for most of the history of the Church, Christians just took this as proof positive that Jesus is the Son of God.

12

Jesus justifies himself to John
Luke 7:18-23

John and Jesus were cousins. They were family. John had stepped back to allow Jesus to shine, but he was also in trouble for his own moral courage. It is possible that this story is set when John is in prison for denouncing the corruption of the local rulers. But it all seems to be going wrong, above all because Jesus is not what John had been expecting. He is not shouty! Where is the fire and the judgement? So, perhaps in despair, John sends messengers to ask Jesus out straight: 'Are you the one who is to come or should we wait for another?' 'Have I got it wrong?' John is asking.

Jesus' reply bears careful reading. It is all life-giving goodness. People are being healed, set free, and reincorporated into society. Especially 'the poor' – those who were at the bottom, on the outside – are being given 'good news'. They are not being judged. The only ones who are being judged are those who take offence at Jesus' loving contact with 'the poor'.

I hope John was encouraged. It was not what he was expecting but it was good news.

One of my frequent talks, especially perhaps at a wedding service where one of the couple has been married before, is to ask people what sort of God they believe in? Do they really believe in a God who likes to say 'no!' 'Thou shalt not . . .' Or a God who likes to say 'yes'? But is that what God is really like? And how might we find the answer to that question?

If we are right as Christians to think of Jesus as our best window into the character of God, then what we have read this week might suggest that God is more like Jesus than John the Baptist. Ready to give people a fresh start. Committed to setting people free from whatever enslaves them. Always life-giving.

Dare we believe this? Or do we really want to believe in a God who likes to say 'no'?

13

The healing of a paralysed man
Luke 5:17-26

Jesus was watched. From quite early on in his public ministry, he got up the noses of the religious authorities. Quite a crowd have come to watch and listen today. Pharisees and teachers of the law and not just the local boys. The top guns from Jerusalem have come as well. Jesus' reputation is spreading quickly. And this sets the context for the miracle story. There are so many people around Jesus, including the 'religious thought-police', that the people who really need to see him are struggling to get to him. (One of the frustrations with the Church is that we spend so much time running the 'machine' that we can't make the time to be with the people who want to meet Jesus . . .)

But the sick man has persistent friends, and they make a hole in the roof to lower him in front of Jesus. That is true love: to wreck a neighbour's roof for love of a friend! But it is all getting terribly public. And then Jesus appears to make it all so much worse by saying something quite inappropriate: 'Friend, your sins are forgiven!'

Now, first, from our perspective, we do not think that this man is paralysed particularly because he is a sinner. This feels like one of those ancient-world-view moments, when Jesus seems especially distant from our age.

But is Jesus playing a longer game? He knows that he has just thrown a match into a box of fireworks by declaring that a man has been forgiven. Only God can do that. Clearly there is something here about Luke inviting us to see the divine in this man Jesus of Nazareth, who has the authority to forgive sins. But I wonder if Jesus was quite so bothered about who was doing the forgiving? This man needed a fresh start, and Jesus gave that to him. Again, is this what God is about – whole salvation?

14

The calling of Levi
Luke 5:27-32

We may be beginning to get a sense of the sort of friends Jesus had. Dodgy. The next one is Levi – a good Jewish name – but he has become a collaborator, collecting taxes at best for a quisling puppet ruler, Herod, and at worst, more distantly, for the oppressive pagan Romans. Politically, socially and religiously isolated. But also good company because he seems to be able to get a lot of his friends together for a feast at short notice. Perhaps he had a good network amongst other 'isolated' people?

Why did Jesus want him as a friend and disciple? We don't know. We are not told. Was there a back-story? Had they met before 'the call' – as with Simon Peter? We don't know. It seems so abrupt that Levi (Matthew?) got up and left everything and followed him. What was it about Jesus that so attracted people? Was it in part that he went out of his way to go home with 'isolated' people? There feels like a parallel here with the story of Jesus going home with Zacchaeus.

Perhaps Levi hated what he was doing but had got stuck with it: not strong enough to work in the fields, clever, made a mistake once and got stuck on the wrong side of the tracks. But he has lots of mates and puts on a great feast which Jesus and his disciples are enjoying, lying around the tables eating and drinking; eating and drinking well, I suspect.

But the watchers are there. The Pharisees and the scribes. Notice that this time they don't complain to Jesus but to Jesus' disciples about their behaviour. 'Why do you eat with these sinners?' Perhaps they can't get close enough to hiss at Jesus. That might mean going right into the heart of this sinners' feast. Perhaps they have already given up with him. But Jesus is listening. And again he comes out with one of those ambiguous sayings that doesn't quite feel like it means what it says.

'Those who are well have no need of a physician, but those who are sick; I have come to call not the righteous but sinners to repentance.' It's worth spelling out the simple stuff before hitting on the ambiguity. Jesus wanted Levi to change. He offered him the chance to change (repent) and Levi grabbed it with both hands. Being a corrupt tax-collector was not what God made Levi to be. God (and Jesus) could see more for him. Jesus did not leave people stuck in bad and damaging situations. And in Luke, salvation is often described in quasi-medical terms. (There is an ancient tradition that Luke himself was a doctor.) So Levi is to be made well holistically.

But we may be struggling both as people and as theologians with some of the rest of the saying. Surely everyone is a 'sinner' in classic Christian theology? Yes. Me too. But I am less sure that this category of original sin was used to make everyone into a sinner in first-century

Israel. I wonder if some of these folk thought they were really not 'sinners'. Technically, the Pharisees kept the Law. As with St Paul, they were technically 'righteous' (Philippians 3:5-9). Was Jesus not interested in them? Examples of him talking deeply with other Pharisees would suggest this was not the case. But perhaps Jesus was inviting them to see that they too were in need of a doctor of the soul? We can't make people see their need of God's love, even if it is obvious that they do need it.

15
Lord of the Sabbath
Luke 6:1-5

I picture Jesus going for a nice 'Sunday afternoon stroll' with his mates and, as we often do when walking through the countryside, picking some of the free-growing fruits around them. A sort of New Testament blackberry picking...

But it wasn't like that. The watchers are there too. Checking how far Jesus and his disciples were walking? And then some of the disciples make it worse by picking some of the heads of grain and getting the edible kernel out. And eating it. Clunk. They have committed an offence under the Old Testament law of the Sabbath, by harvesting. We might be tempted to say 'duh' and disregard the weight of this accusation, but Jesus is struggling for his Jewish credentials against people who (will) do him harm if they regard him as unsound. Jews had died rather than give up their Sabbath obedience. This was sensitive territory.

Jesus does two things. First, he quotes the scriptures, reminding the watchers that there is good precedent for breaking the law when human need requires. He reminds the watchers of the story of David and his guerrilla soldiers being given illegally the holy bread from the very presence of Yahweh because they were famished (1 Samuel 21:4-6). It is quite a heavyweight response but makes the point!

He then goes much further. 'The Son of Man is lord of the Sabbath.' Who? What? The son of man is one of the most elusive of Jesus' self-descriptions. It has messianic overtones (Daniel 7:13, 14), but not straightforwardly. And it seems to hint more at being one of 'us' than being 'Son of God'. But nonetheless, this humble messiah is still 'lord of the sabbath', able to take decisions about how it was to be observed, or not. This little phrase, 'son of man', goes right back to the earliest parts of the gospel tradition. We need have no doubts that Jesus talked about himself like this. And yet, on the basis of this mysterious title which he took to himself, he sets aside hundreds of years of Israelite sabbatarian tradition. There is an intriguing sort of authority at work here.

16

The Calling of the Twelve
Luke 6:12-19

The Gospels are full of little phrases which we skip over. They sound 'religious', so we don't stop to feel their reality. Jesus needs to choose the core inner group of his disciples, whom he will train up – leave in charge when he goes? We may take this for granted, but I wonder if it was a difficult decision. Jesus was going to disappoint some people. So he goes out on his own to a mountain to pray, all night. I have never done this. I guess most of us haven't. I have been up (little) mountains, by day. They can be scary enough even then, but at night, on my own? And in Jesus' day with wild animals around. This is serious praying. Difficult decisions.

Jesus makes the difficult decision and calls the Twelve Apostles. Given the symbolic weight that is given to them, I am intrigued that we know so little about them, including even the exact list of names! God knows who they were. And as we have already seen, they are a mixed bunch and were not to prove the most reliable of disciples and friends.

Now that's another bit of reality. Did Jesus not know what he was doing? How could he (of all people!) have got it wrong, not least about Judas? We believe that, in the providence of God, even this choice had its deep purpose, but Jesus did not have a crystal ball. He had to make the best case judgements – in prayer.

And then he comes down from the mountain top with his new team and Luke shows us that he is straight back to work, preaching and healing. Giving out. His disciples should have been in no doubt about what they were signing up for . . . Did they really understand? Do we? In all its riskiness?

17

Jesus heals a centurion's servant
Luke 7:1-10

Jesus is back in Capernaum. It seems to have become a sort of home from home. But there is a little local problem. A local centurion has a slave who is 'dear to him', who is dying. It is probable that this man is a Herodian centurion, but he is still a professional soldier, trained to lead from the front and kill as required. I met some senior NCOs when I was younger. They frightened me silly! Hugely reliable but tough, tough. I imagine this man like that, but more so.

But he has a slave who is dear to him. Slaves were property. They could be treated any which way. But this hard professional soldier cares for this slave. Some scholars have seen in the language strong hints at a particular sort of relationship. That in itself might have been unusual. What is perhaps even more unusual is that the centurion reaches out to Jesus. But he does it indirectly, by sending a message via the local Jewish village elders. I wonder how they felt! We can hear some of their anxiety in the way they plead with Jesus to do something. So Jesus decides to do a home visit.

But before he can get there, the centurion's nerve cracks. He tells Jesus not to come. Not because Jesus is not worthy to come to his house – which would have been the expected attitude – but because he, the centurion, is not worthy. And the centurion says this because he has some sense of who Jesus is, of Jesus' authority. People who carry real authority recognise it in others. This centurion sees something more in Jesus. And Jesus is astonished, that a pagan soldier has such faith.

As I am writing this, I am thinking of some of the people I have met, who don't 'come to church' but whose faith has astonished me. I have two questions for myself. 'Why don't I meet more people like this in my regular parish work, and what might we do to help them to feel connected to the community of Jesus' disciples?'

18

Jesus meets a sinful woman
Luke 7:36-50

It's too easy to portray the Pharisees as the 'bad guys'. In this story, one of them has invited Jesus to dinner. They are on first-name terms. But it is not a cosy dinner party, it is a public event and an unwelcome guest arrives. A prostitute. It is difficult to read the brief description of her in any other way.

I don't think I have ever had a lengthy conversation with a prostitute. I was propositioned once. It took her two goes to get me to realise what she was offering. It was an uncomfortable encounter. And we know too much about the realities of prostitution to read this story romantically. This is a woman who lives on the margin of her community, vulnerable, ostracised, used, but used to using her body.

And she uses her body to express her sadness and her longing to live differently. She weeps on Jesus' feet. Washes them. Anoints them with expensive perfume. And dries them with her hair. It is extraordinarily tender and sensual.

Jesus is not remotely uncomfortable. Quite the opposite. When Simon the Pharisee starts to complain, Jesus affirms her behaviour in detail, including that she kissed his feet.[7]

If there is one Gospel story in Luke that makes me love Jesus, it is this one. This earthy, accepting, brave spirituality. This is who he was. This is why the folk who were on the edge of things loved him and why those at the centre of religious power loathed him.

So often the Church has been the very opposite of Jesus. How can we get Jesus into our DNA?

---

7. I used this text as a test case for how the different historical exegetes handled a difficult text. The Fathers extensively allegorised the text so that, for example, the woman became the Church. See Just, pp.124ff. The Reformation exegetes spent more time discussing the nature of repentance. See Kreitzer, pp.162ff. But I was very moved to read the most positive account of the woman's perspective, written by a woman exegete, Catherina Regina von Greiffenberg: 'The salvific seed of woman (Jesus) did not reject women, refusing to be served by them. Since he dignified them by his own being made flesh of a woman, he therefore also found them worthy to witness his death. He wanted to begin his emerging from this sex and to end it in their company. He knew that he has caressed and pressed the ardour of love into them and granted fidelity to them in particular. Thus he meant to enjoy the noble fruit of this tree that his right hand had planted and to receive the sweet perfume of the love of this true-hearted refresher before his suffering . . .' It is surely a tragedy that the Church had to wait so long for such exegesis and that it has been such a silenced voice.

19
Joseph
Luke 2:1-7

God's great project needs all sorts of people. All of us indeed. Some will be up front, in the limelight, perhaps even getting much of the credit. Others will be behind the scenes, not saying much, but crucial to putting on the show.

If you are reading this during Lent, then this should be a Sunday and, slightly randomly, I thought we should think about Joseph today. (The trigger is that we are thinking about Mary next week.) He is an ambiguous figure in the Christian tradition. He comes and goes quite quickly. There is nothing about Joseph himself after Jesus is aged 12. Tradition tells us that he had died by the time Jesus reached adulthood and he is often portrayed as an older man. Jesus is sometimes described as Joseph's son and sometimes as Mary's. That may suggest that Joseph had been dead some while before the public events in the life of Jesus, or that there was still a legacy of suspicion over Jesus' birth. Jesus is often described as Mary's son (unusual in this culture) not Joseph's, because there was doubt about his parentage.

It is Matthew who tells us the stories about Joseph's agonising. In Luke, Joseph is a protector and provider figure. I remember still with a little glow of pride being chosen to play Joseph in the primary school nativity play, and having to walk around the stage knocking on a series of imaginary doors, only to be turned away, all the while with my arm around Mary. I felt very grown up. In my memory, it helped that Mary was pretty! But I felt very protective. I think that is how Luke wants us to imagine Joseph.

But as I said, he is a deeply ambiguous figure. He is the father figure but is of course not the father. And for Christians for whom the nativity stories strain their capacity to believe, how is Joseph not the father? How do we celebrate his role if we are struggling with believing the virginal conception? Indeed, how do we celebrate this messy and beautiful story without simply suppressing our questions, especially as the creative retelling of the Nativity Story increases its scope every year. (Last year I heard of children being cast as crabs in a nativity play – delightful, but what?) So Joseph becomes for us modern Christians a very ambiguous figure. And so we stop thinking about him, which is a tragedy, because there is depth here.

Briefly, and using the simplest of theological language, if we believe in the Incarnation, then we are asked to believe that Joseph becomes a surrogate father for the Son of God, an adoptive parent for over 12 years. We are right at the limit of what we can say theologically, responsibly, now, but we might say that God entrusted his Son to Joseph for protection and upbringing. It is an act of extraordinary humility. It demanded immense grace from Joseph. He seemed to have been able to give it and the result was Jesus of Nazareth. Not bad for someone whose speaking part is almost non-existent.

20

The Lucan Beatitudes
Luke 6:20-23

It's interesting that it is Matthew's version of the Beatitudes which is better known in the Church. They are longer and fuller. They do not include the 'Woes', which we will read tomorrow, and that makes them a little more comfortable. But the version in Luke is earthier and more immediate – more practical? 'Blessed are you who are poor because the Kingdom is yours *now*. Blessed are you who are hungry *now*. You will be fed. Blessed are you who are crying *now*. You will laugh.'

We are back with the Jesus everyone loves to love. The topsy-turvy, world-turning-upside-down, idealistic Jesus. The Jesus Gandhi admired. The Jesus whose ideas we seem unable to put into practice. But this Jesus is, in fact, promising justice. Those who are hungry now – really hungry, tummies aching, bellies swollen with malnutrition – you will be fed. Those who are crying now – weeping for a lost life, in suffering, in fear – you will laugh. It is both a promise (yet to be fulfilled) and a command. It is indeed nothing short of revolution. In a world where people are still hungry, we are breaking Jesus' simple command. This is simple stuff. It should be. We should and can just make this happen.

But there is a puzzle. Jesus says to the poor – the actually poor not just the 'poor in spirit'– the Kingdom (of God) is yours *now*. What did he mean? It can't have felt like that for those living by begging in the streets of Jerusalem. Is Matthew right with his more 'spiritualising' version? Are the poor blessed because they bring blessings to others who are drawn to care for them? (A traditional way of interpreting this verse.) Again, I suspect it does not feel like that. Are the poor blessed with the Kingdom because they have to depend on God? I've seen the simple joy in poor African faces, so there is some truth there – but African parents want their children to be well-fed, well-educated and healthy. Real poverty is not a blessing.

I cannot offer a simple explanation of what Jesus meant, but I wonder if it is to do with what we used to call 'God's preferential option for the poor', 'God's bias to the poor'. God really is on the side of the oppressed. That's who God is fighting for. That's who God is building his Kingdom for. The clue is, these were the people Jesus spent most time with. Now that is a blessing.

21
The Woes
Luke 6:24-26

I find these some of the most frightening verses in Luke's Gospel. Because I am (fairly) rich and well-fed and (mostly) happy. We live in a society, and even more a world, where there are very sharp differentials in wealth. Some people have obscene amounts of money. Other do not have enough to live on. In the parishes where I work, some children are hungry in the school holidays because they are deprived of the regular free school meals. I know what it is to be short of stuff and even more to be envious of those who have their own (second) home and so on, but I am not poor or hungry. I do not know that churning sense of anger and frustration and also despair at not being able to provide for those I love. I do not long for justice – by which I mean not some abstract justice for someone else, but a fair chance for me and my family.

Jesus' 'woes' (warnings) in Luke require a lot of careful thinking. They assume that there is not just an unequal society but an unjust one, where those who are wealthy and happy now are so because someone else has lost out to them. Our society may not obviously look like that – though why were the trainers I bought for my holiday so cheap? They assume that there will be a divine 'putting right' of injustice, in some 'next world' where those who have suffered now will get justice and blessing, but those who have been rich now will not be blessed again. We may not quite see life in this world and in the next like this. We have become wary about speaking about the next life as a compensation for troubles in this one. 'Jam tomorrow.' But it is worth pondering that almost all of the world's major religions foresee judgement after death, and recompense. Indeed, if there is never going to be any recompense for the innocent suffering we see daily, then this world is unbearable. One of the good things about recent theological thinking has been the clarity with which the 'jam tomorrow' view of heaven has stopped being a way of saying to people, 'so stop grumbling that you have no jam today'. We know God wants 'jam today' for everyone . . .

So I want to say that there is not a simple 'so there' to be read from these 'woes'. Jesus is not telling me that the blessings I have now are all I am ever likely to get eternally. But if these words do frighten me, then that is a good thing, because it makes me think about the things I have, the food I eat, the life I live, and ask: 'Are they at the expense of others?' One day I will have to look into his eyes and there will be no hiding place for my selfishness.

22

Love

Luke 6:27-38

Each of the Gospel writers gives us a particular angle on Jesus, like a tour guide showing us one aspect of a beautiful and complex sculpture. I think these verses in Luke's Gospel are at the heart of Luke's understanding of Jesus. They are familiar words of Jesus, but Luke writes them down this way in the light of his knowledge and understanding of the Passion of Jesus. This was not just idealism. It was tough love in a brutal world.

So Jesus in Luke's Gospel prays, 'Father forgive them, they do not know what they are doing.' Jesus in Luke shows the mercy which he speaks of here, as he says to the dying robber: 'Today you will be with me in paradise.'

One of the tasks we set ourselves in our little book is to see through Jesus to God. This is one of the clearest passages in Luke where we can do that. Jesus says, 'Be merciful' – 'because God your father is merciful'. This is Jesus taking us to a window into the nature of God and saying, 'Look and see, this is how God really is and so this is how we can and should be'. Non-judgemental. Ready to forgive. Above all, generous. It is quite a risk to live like this and we may find, from time to time, that we lose out or are even taken for a ride. But if God is really like this then we can't live any other way, not least because this is how God is with us.

And again, as Luke knew when he wrote this, we see these values lived out by Jesus in the most extreme of circumstances. It can be done. And when it is done, it is transformative.

23
Logs and specks
Luke 6:39-42

What is Jesus doing when he talks like this? He is part of the Wisdom Tradition which forms one of the great strands of the Hebrew Bible. Some of that tradition was shared with other Near Eastern cultures. We can imagine all sorts of teachers offering this piece of simple hard-hitting wisdom about hypocrisy. Perhaps it can remind us that God's wisdom is spread widely in God's world, and here Jesus is joining in that wisdom.

But what is Jesus doing? It seems to me that so much of Jesus' ministry was about subverting those who thought they were in the right, particularly the religious and indeed those with religious power. So why is Jesus doing this? Is it because he thinks that everyone is a sinner and so wants to bring everyone down? This might be the classic view of the Church as found, for example, in the *Book of Common Prayer*, where we are all 'miserable sinners'. So that we are all reduced to repentance in the face of a holy God.

Or is this really a more specific piece of teaching, designed to subvert the self-righteous? This could be part of the wider scheme of reducing everyone to humility before God, but a straightforward reading of these words is that it is about tackling religious and moral hypocrisy: claiming to be, thinking we are, what we are not – better than others. This is a corrupt self-deceiving lie and Jesus will not let us get away with it. I think this piece of teaching is targeted at those who think of themselves like this.

I worry sometimes that those of us inside the Church slip very easily into thinking that we are better than those outside and that this makes us insensitive to those 'outside' the Church. If we think that 'we have it' then we will find ourselves talking, talking down, not listening to those who don't. And we wonder why people don't want to listen when a conversation has this dynamic ... Perhaps Jesus had a foreboding of what was coming. Or perhaps he really just could not bear hypocrisy.

24

The house on the rock
Luke 6:46-49

'Gentle Jesus, meek and mild.' Only he wasn't. As we have seen, he was not afraid to challenge the authorities. And he had a strong sense of his own authority. This is a very famous image that Jesus uses to describe his own teaching. Luke, like Matthew, puts it at the end of a block of Jesus' teaching, so we are left in no doubt that we are to take this seriously.

So seriously that we *do it*. We think that we live in a world where we are dominated by information input and are infused with cynicism, so we are resistant to guidance. I suspect this is part of the human condition, especially when the guidance is uncomfortable, difficult for us to hear and do. But Jesus wants us to trust him enough to do it. To do the loving and forgiving, because it is reliable teaching and he is reliable.

We should note this confidence. Partly because what Jesus is advocating is very challenging, counter-cultural, risky. So to command people to follow it is both to demand much of them but also to express a deep confidence. Occasionally as a preacher I get an attack of the wobbles. Who am I to say this? But Jesus does not have an attack of the wobbles even when he is being as radical as this.

Because we need to say again this is not obviously rock-like teaching, to love and forgive. Jesus is asking us to take a risk but he also said consistently: this is what God is like and so this really is how the world is. Do we believe him?

25

Jesus and John
Luke 7:31-35

Jesus is serious, but not *that* serious. Again he draws this contrast between himself and John the Baptist. John came lamenting and preaching judgement. Jesus came partying. Jesus is not putting John down. Both are people of Wisdom. But it is striking that Jesus portrays himself as a party animal with dodgy friends. Indeed, such a party animal that he can be accused of being a drunkard. I have read this passage often but I have never before heard that word, that Jesus was accused of being a 'drunkard' and that he had heard it, perhaps felt the contempt of it, and then turned it back on his accusers.

If we were to read this in a classic Christian theological way, notice what we would be saying: that when God came to earth in human form he was accused of being a drunkard. It is important to be hard-headedly serious at this moment. Drunkenness, especially persistent drunkenness which slides into alcoholism, is not funny and is dangerous for the person and those close to them. But this is not what Jesus is saying. He is describing how he spent his time and perhaps especially the people he enjoyed being with, partying with sinners.

This is not what I might have expected of God incarnate and clearly it was not what his contemporaries expected of the Messiah. But why do we not expect God to be a party animal? A question to ponder, because I don't think that we do. But if we are right in asking ourselves what Jesus might teach us about God, then this is worth pondering, because it might change our deepest gut assumptions about God, and about the sort of people God wants us to be.

The sadness is that neither solemnity nor joy won people over in Jesus' day. What about us?

26
The Magnificat
Luke 1:46-56

I grew up on Evensong and have often sung the Magnificat (which is the Latin name for this song of Mary) to ethereal melodies. These days I do more listening than singing! The effect is both uplifting and calming. But I have a bad conscience about this, because the Magnificat is not other-worldly or calming; it is a song of judgement and revolution, more suitable for the conference of a left-wing political party.

The first few verses – and Luke ordered this so that it sounded like one of the great hymns of praise from the Hebrew Bible (Hannah's song, for example, found in 1 Samuel 2:1-10) – are full of the rejoicing and praise for God of a humble girl blessed with an unimaginable blessing. You may be reading this on Mothering Sunday, so you may have images of a demure Mary in your mind . . . But then half way through (verse 51), it begins to sound more like a judgement from one of the Hebrew prophets. God has judged the proud for their pride and confused them in their own thinking. Perhaps their own pride will bring about their downfall – *hubris*. The powerful (and corrupt) have had political power taken from them by God's power and the hungry are now fed, whilst the rich are sent empty away. And all this is described as faithfulness to Abraham.

This could be deeply puzzling, especially in a Church of England cathedral surrounded by monuments to the rich and powerful, but only if we keep thinking of the Magnificat, and of Jesus, and of God, as other-worldly. As we have already learned, Jesus came to bring justice, including social and political justice. In his day, the rich and powerful – and the two went together – could so manipulate things that they became ever more rich and powerful, normally at the expense of the vast majority of the population whose labour produced the produce that created their wealth. Sounds familiar . . .

Jesus came teaching that this was not the way in God's Kingdom and he lived like this too. If we take Jesus seriously as a window into God then we will be drawn into God's work of establishing justice. We may now often be able to do this peacefully, but that does not stop it being a powerful change that will be powerfully resisted.

Is this the sort of God we want to believe in? Or do we want to drift back into Evensong?

27

The parable of the sower
Luke 8:4-15

This most famous of the parables has a deeply uncomfortable framing. We can understand the meaning of the parable. God's word is offered to different people. Some people seem to be impervious and in this version of the parable it is the devil who then snatches the message away. Others respond with initial enthusiasm but, when the heat comes on, they lose their faith. Others again start the journey of faith, but life – with its joys and troubles – stifles the faith. Whereas others do respond and, in one of Jesus' delightful exaggerations, they produce one hundred times the fruit. This is an amazing return for a farmer and is a clear sign of Jesus' confidence in human capacity to respond to God and do amazing things with and for God.

But the uncomfortable framing is when Jesus says that he tells this parable so that people will not understand easily. Surely Jesus would want people to understand him as easily as possible? But is life and faith as simple as that? Sometimes Jesus speaks with utter clarity. Other times he speaks in such a way as to invite, even require, a response. This seems to connect with how it is with God in life. Sometimes shocking clarity, sometimes hiddenness. A straightforward reading of this text would suggest that this is God's will, to block people from hearing. But we must interpret this in the light of Jesus' many uses of words like 'all' and 'everyone' and his constant invitation, especially to the vulnerable, to go with him.

However, there is a sad counterpoint to this which, as a vicar, I feel very deeply. There is a mystery about how people respond to the invitation to faith. I understand that for some people the language of faith has no purchase on them. What is harder to understand are the folk who experience the love of God, who begin the journey of faith, but who drop away because the heat comes on, or the distractions gather round – even folk who have been deeply embedded within the Church. It seems to me sometimes that no one is safe from the loss of faith. That is of course not the same thing as the loss of God. God does not lose us.

28

Jairus' daughter and the woman with the haemorrhage
Luke 8:40-56

I find this is one of the most beautiful of the miracle stories in Luke. It is full of pathos. Jairus, the leader of the synagogue, comes and falls at Jesus' feet, in desperation. Notice that Jesus has just 'returned'. To where? Is it to Capernaum? Or even Nazareth? It may be significant because, if it is either of these two places, then these are synagogues where Jesus is already unpopular. What was at stake for the leader of one of these synagogues to come and throw himself at the feet of Jesus? Nothing less than the life of his only child, his daughter. Professional history went through a phase of thinking that people in the past lost so many children that they had different attitudes to grief: that they did not form affectionate relationships with their children in case they died. I was never convinced by this, and Jairus clearly shows us the opposite. He is distraught that he might lose his only child, who is of course a daughter and so less valuable . . . but not to Jairus. He loves her deeply, and will sacrifice his public position if it will save her. Desperation causes him to reach out.

As it does for the woman with the haemorrhage. Intriguingly, she has been ill for 12 years (the age of Jairus' daughter . . .). She is desperate. She is now, we are to imagine, impoverished by the failed medical treatment. She is presumably also humiliated. (The whole village would of course have known.) And shunned: she was ritually unclean and many of her fellow villagers would not have wanted to let her near, let alone actually touch her. But she is so desperate she takes the risk of trying to touch Jesus. But even in the press of a crowd she cannot bring herself to touch him directly or to ask him to touch her, and so she surreptitiously touches just the fringe of his clothes. 'He will never feel that, and I may be cured,' she may have thought. But Jesus does notice. He stops, and demands to know who has touched him. In the end, Peter tries to reason with him, pointing out truthfully (and probably 'patiently') that, in a jostling crowd, anyone might have touched him. And this triggers a window into how Jesus experienced his personal ministry of healing. He noticed that 'power had gone out from him'. It is so tantalising. Was this a physical sensation? Or emotional or spiritual? Was it automatic —had power gone out from him but without his agreement? Did that happen only if someone of faith touched him? And was it essential for there to be touch? I don't know the answer to any of these questions. However we *now* understand Jesus' miraculous powers – and Luke clearly believed in them and wanted his readers to believe in them – there was even in Luke's account some puzzlement about the miracles. For not only did Jesus heal the woman, he will go on to raise the dead child, in the face of direct scepticism – 'they laughed at him'. Like us, people in the ancient world knew that in reality the dead stayed dead. But Jesus raises the child to life. (There is perhaps a significant point here in that Jesus says she is 'sleeping' whereas, in other resurrections, he acknowledges that the person is clearly dead.) And then suggests that they give her something to eat because, whatever journey she has been on, she needs nourishment.

I love these stories because of the sheer human tenderness involved. A desperate outcast woman is publicly restored. A desperate grieving father is reunited with his daughter. This is the Jesus I love. But I have to note that it is precisely Jesus as both tender pastor and powerful healer that I love. Man and God.

29
The feeding of the five thousand
Luke 9:12-17

I remember a secondary school lesson on this story. (I was a grammar school boy, but RE was not taken seriously in those days. How times have improved.) In fact, I have a very clear memory of the gist of the lesson. It was taken for granted that it could not have been an actual miracle – Jesus causing the bread and fish to expand in an extraordinary and unnatural way whilst being distributed – but the explanation offered was that Jesus so inspired the crowd with his love and faith and expectation of generosity, that they shared their packed lunches too. I was a 'keen Christian' at the time and of course privately denounced such heresy, but the idea has stuck for 40 years. That is interesting in itself.

I have to confess to you, dear reader, that this is one of the miracles that I struggle to understand. I can believe in Resurrection. I can believe in healing. In other words I can believe in divine power changing human bodies – cells, atoms, blood, muscles, heart – but I cannot imagine how this miracle worked. How were loaves and fishes expanded? Did it happen all at once? Did the disciples see it happening as they put their hands into the baskets to take out the next portion? I don't know, and notice that Luke does not tell us anything in detail of how the miracle happened. (Nor do the other Gospel writers.)

I wonder if that is important. That we are not supposed to worry away at the detail but rather at the point of the miracle story: people in need were generously fed by a combination of God's bounty and human faith and generosity. It is a symbolic story. But does that mean I don't need to believe it actually happened? This was clearly a well-known story in the Jesus tradition. It features with variants as well as intriguing details (the spring grass in John) in all the Gospels. It mattered to the Early Church and it mattered to the Gospel writers, perhaps because it was such a clear sign of the Kingdom arriving, with its hints of the creation of a new Israel (twelve baskets of leftovers collected).

But is it true? I both think and believe it to be true, though I have no idea 'how' it happened and have rather more sympathy for my old RE teacher now! But what strikes me is that it moves me precisely in the way that our last passage moves me: Jesus is caring for people in deep and pressing need. And to answer that need he is both human – he empathises – and divine – he transforms. I am being forced to see that for Luke the two are inseparable, in a way that was perhaps not so true for my old RE teacher.

30
Peter's Confession
Luke 9:18-22

Notice that, in Luke, we have moved straight from the feeding of the five thousand to Peter's great confession. Because we so often read the Gospels in short segments a week apart, we don't get an insight-generating sense of how the Gospel writers constructed their texts. We probably imagine – if we think of it at all – that Luke wrote things down in the order he thought they happened. I am really not sure that was how Luke worked, and certainly here he has a slightly different order from Mark and Matthew. I am confident that this is because Luke regarded the feeding of the five thousand as the miracle that confirmed Jesus' status, so that it follows naturally to hear Peter's great confession of faith, which structurally is such a profound turning point in the Gospels, because from now on Jesus looks explicitly to Jerusalem and the Cross and Resurrection.

We too have spent several weeks now with Luke's Jesus, and I have suggested in the last two reflections that, to understand how Luke understood Jesus, we have needed to understand that Luke saw Jesus as divine as well as human. It is really important not to read back into Luke the full rigours of later creedal Christianity, just as it is important to recognise that the Early Church was convinced it was being faithful to Luke and indeed all its scriptures when it pronounced Jesus to be fully God and fully human.

But what do we make of this Jesus, and indeed of this whole project? It is one thing for us to understand that this was how Luke saw Jesus, but do we have to follow him, and Peter, in making this decision too?

The writing of new studies of the life of Jesus, understandably, never ceases. But I hope we have moved on from the view that he was simply a good man, who was misunderstood and then misinterpreted and misrepresented by the Church, so that he became this divine figure floating six inches above reality and contradiction. Even given the complexities in the move from the actual events of the life of Jesus of Nazareth to the written account in Luke's Gospel, a real person shines through. A person who is tender-hearted as well as passionate about justice, and committed to helping everyone, but especially the most vulnerable and marginalised, to know that God is for them and with them. It is illuminating to ponder what Luke himself brought to the telling of this story – concern for women, possibly some medical expertise, a Gentile perspective – but in the end it is not convincing that Luke is a more significant person than Jesus, not least because we meet (mostly) the same Jesus in all the Gospels. In reading Luke we meet Jesus.

And in reading Luke we meet a Jesus who is tender, passionate, funny and rebellious but also mysterious, frightening and powerful in ways that are, I find, baffling. Let me put this simply. I find Jesus of Nazareth as presented in Luke's Gospel deeply attractive as a human being. I wish I was more like him. But I know that I cannot be too like him because he is bafflingly different. He is God-like in his power. And I cannot, even if I interpret Luke, as I must, as a twenty-first-century person, cut this part of Jesus out of the Gospel. The divine and the human are, as we have seen, inextricable in this story. If that is the case and if it is reliable, then I may be forced, enabled, to see through Jesus to God. As Peter did.

31

The Transfiguration
Luke 9:28-36

In the last reflection, I tried to offer a reasoned way of thinking which took us from Luke's Jesus to God. When confronted by the Transfiguration, I feel the need to write differently. This goes beyond being baffled, to being in a different universe to the one I normally inhabit.

I understand the theological point that Luke is making, and which sometimes the Western Church has found to be too rich a diet: that somehow 'inside' Jesus is this divine Person who is revealed in this extraordinary event, as if a veil is withdrawn from him, so that the glory which has been constrained inside is allowed to break free, momentarily. I like the way the story is told so we have the contrast between the deep symbolism of the presence of Moses and Elijah, the great figures of the Hebrew Bible in terms of Law and Prophecy, and the familiar clumsiness of Peter, who wants to make three huts so that they will stay longer – for ever? He so does not want this moment of heavenly glory to end. I am moved by what will come next, when Jesus has to come down the mountain and sort out the frailties and failings of his disciples.

But I am, above all, simply wanting to sit and be quiet in the face of the transfigured Jesus. I do not know what the glory of God is like. Here the glory of God takes what is familiar – Jesus' normal appearance – and shines through it. Is this light shining out? Is it meant to make us think that divine reality, divine glory, is utterly different from ours? Is this divine glory around us often, but unseen, hidden from us? Again, I don't know the answer to any of these questions but in Jesus these two realities seem to merge together, seamlessly. Is he a sort of bridge for us?

And there is an encouragement for us to think this. St Paul, perhaps picking up on his understanding of this story, writes that we have this same glory in our hearts, and it enables us to see the glory that was in the face of Jesus (2 Corinthians 4:6).

32
Failed disciples
Luke 9:37-43

'Gentle Jesus, meek and mild' never got impatient with anyone ... Not true. Today's passage reads like an all too human reaction. Jesus is coming down from literally a mountain top experience, but he arrives back in the 'real world' to find his disciples failing. It looks like Jesus is confronted by the desperate father of an epileptic boy. Presumably the disciples he had left behind had been praying and trying to exorcise this demon out of the child but had failed, and the child was left at the mercy of this terrible affliction.

I wonder where the problem lay? It looks like it was with the disciples. Did they lack faith? Or is it a wider problem? Is it the whole community which is 'faithless and perverse'? But whatever the truth of that, Jesus' heartfelt frustration is that he wants to be free of such people. Of course, Jesus then goes on to meet the boy who is fitting, sends the evil spirit away, and returns the boy safe and well to his father. And in characteristic Lucan language, all 'were astounded at the greatness of God'.

Now one line of interpretation – which we hear elsewhere in the Gospels – is that the healing was delayed until Jesus arrived, precisely to bring glory to

God through Jesus. But the text does not say that. It is much more uncomfortable. The disciples were failing. Jesus gets really impatient. (Fascinating that this little story was remembered and thought important enough to be woven into the Gospel at this crucial stage . . .)

This takes us to a deep question. The Church quite quickly began to talk of Jesus as 'sinless' and this became a matter of doctrine. Whilst fully human he was also completely perfect, as befitted the Son of God incarnate. The divine could not be mixed with the sinful. I wonder if this is helpful? This language seems to make Jesus' humanity unbelievable. So different from us as to be alien to us. I prefer an impatient and frustrated Jesus. And I am not sure that this is sinful in any very profound sense anyway. It is simply human. He is on a high and then has to face frustrating and painful reality. I can empathise with that frustration.

But of course he does not give up, either on the boy or on the disciples. Perhaps that is the difference. That I am tempted to give up on people. Indeed, I have done so and suspect I will do so again. But Jesus doesn't. Is this a helpful window into what a faithful God might be like?

33

An old man, Simeon, meets the baby Jesus
Luke 2:25-35

If you are reading this during Lent, then today is 'Passion Sunday' when we begin to look firmly towards the Cross. So it may feel odd to be going back to the beginning of Jesus' life. This is a reading telling the story of Mary and Joseph taking the baby Jesus to the Temple in Jerusalem to be dedicated. They were fulfilling part of the ancient Mosaic Law regarding the birth of an eldest son.

This is another of the passages in Luke where Luke has told a story so it sounds like a story from the Hebrew Bible. So Simeon delivers his prophecy in the polished prose poetry which we have come to call the *Nunc Dimittis,* the Latin for 'now you are dismissing . . .'. It is the second canticle in Evensong in the *Book of Common Prayer* and I have sung and said it hundreds of times. We also read these words at the end of a funeral service in church, especially for an active Christian believer, as we carry their coffin out of church for burial. It is a closing celebration of their faith, and a plea for peaceful rest.

That is very fitting, because these are the words of an old man who has spent his life longing for God to liberate Israel. And in this new-born, Simeon sees God's promise fulfilled. The *Nunc Dimittis* oozes an end to weary waiting but also a readiness to let go. However we imagine the original encounter, in Luke's telling of it we see an old man still full of the Spirit who is able to see God's deliverance in this tiny human life. Church and family are two of the places where we still mix across the age groups and are enriched by that. We see it happening here.

But as with the *Magnificat*, this story has painful ingredients. Simeon finishes it by looking at Mary. He warns her that this child will bring division. People will have to choose and some will be hurt by their choices. And she too will be hurt, wounded by grief, as she watches her son die in agony on a cross.

It is right that the Church calls these days 'Passiontide'. They are full of suffering and deep emotion. Jesus is fully part of the passion of the human condition. He is not immune from any of this. If we allow ourselves to imagine that he really is 'God' going through this, then it becomes more extraordinary. Now is not the time to enter into the ancient and complex theological debates of whether 'God' can suffer. But Jesus did, for sure. And Jesus takes us into the heart of God.

And of course Mary suffers too. Our hearts will ache for her as she stands bravely at the foot of the Cross. It is right that the Church has so often looked to her in love and respect. The ancient Church called her the *theotokos*, the God-bearer. The God-bearer may have wept with joy at the birth of her son. We will soon see the God-bearer weep at his death.

Salvation is costly.

34

The Good Samaritan
Luke 10:25-37

This is another one of the 'Sunday School' lessons embedded in Luke's Gospel, which includes some of the most beautiful *and* challenging of Jesus' parables. Beautiful because it's about sheer compassion and great generosity and that touches us simply. But challenging because of the identity of the good person. He is a Samaritan.

Let's work with that for a bit until we come back again to the meaning of the parable. The parable is shocking. The victim needs help. The first two people ought to help him. Both are religious professionals. And of course the parable is directed to a religious professional. The one who does help is a heretic (a churchy, not a Jewish word) and also mixed-race. In other words, the least likely person to help, in orthodox eyes.

So this parable is not just about acting compassionately but also about expectations, or rather subverting expectations. The lawyer ought to have known what is expected of an orthodox believer. But why did Jesus make him so uncomfortable? Was it in part to puncture some self-righteousness Jesus detected in the lawyer? And of course, the lawyer has no option but to affirm the Samaritan, the despised untouchable half-breed, as someone who keeps the greatest of the commandments.

So this parable is perhaps not fundamentally about simply being a Good Person, the kind of person the English apparently love ('he would do anything for anyone' is a frequent catchphrase I hear on a funeral visit). Rather, it is about not assuming that publicly religious people will be good: something those of us in the Church of all theological traditions need to be reminded of again and again. We can all fall prey to self-righteousness whether we are good social activists, good born-again Bible-believers or good sacramental catholics. It is about looking for goodness where goodness is really found, not where we think it should be found.

Why does Jesus teach this parable? Why does subverting human expectations of goodness matter to him? Is it because when a human being or group assumes they are right, their behaviour can become wicked and cut them off from God?

35

The Lord's Prayer
Luke 11:1-4

This is a uniquely important text because it is one of the very few examples we have of the content of Jesus' prayer, especially when he was teaching others how to pray. So, what did Jesus teach his disciples to pray for (broadly speaking, because the versions of the Lord's Prayer in Matthew and Luke are a bit different)?

He taught them to pray to God as their Father, that God's rule would come on earth.

Whilst it was not unique to pray to God as Father, it was radical in the extent to which Jesus prayed in this way and taught others to pray like this. And also the intimate language which Jesus used – *abba*, father, even 'Dad'. This is an intriguing combination, the language of fatherhood and the language of kingship. It is God as Father who is coming to rule on earth.

And what does it look like when the values of God as Father are lived out on earth?

God's name is honoured, respected, shown to be holy and weighty. In other words, God matters enough for people to do as God intends. And what does this look like? It looks like basic human need is met. There is enough bread to eat. It looks like forgiveness and humility and reconciliation within and between people. It looks like people are kept from times of suffering, of testing. To risk being simplistic, this sounds like good fatherly care.

But when we pray the prayer like this, it doesn't sound very churchy. Like you, I have prayed this prayer more times than I could calculate. Most often in church at almost every service I attend. Quite often in schools with young children who can just about get their tongues around the words, let alone figure out what it means. And sometimes at a hospital bedside or even at a death bed. It is a badge of identity for Christians, a comfort, words I say without being aware what I have said, and words where every syllable counts. But I have not thought about them as being as intensely practical as this before: food, reconciliation, protection. Is this what Jesus thought God's Kingdom was like? Intensely this-worldly? It is ironic then that we tend to make it a very churchy prayer. And beyond ironic that we pray it without getting how practical it should be. So if fatherly care is practical, what are we doing as the father's children?

36
Ask, and it shall be given
Luke 11:5-13

I find this passage very difficult. I should love it. It is one of Jesus' classic sets of sayings about prayer, full of confident reassurance. 'Ask, and it will be given to you . . .' But life does not feel like that. I quite often read these verses at funerals when, as well as giving thanks for someone who has been a good father, I am suggesting that we can understand God as good father in the light of what we have known of good fatherhood (the principle of analogy – we build from what we know, human fathering, to what we cannot see, divine fathering). But I also read these verses conscious that a family may have prayed desperately for a healing that never came. This is a fact and, as Christians, we do neither ourselves nor anyone else any favours by pretending that prayer is sometimes (often?) not answered in the way that we have asked. There are of course all sorts of wise things we can say about 'unanswered prayer': God works with human beings, not over them; this must be a reliable universe where playgrounds don't turn into marshmallow when children fall over; and God knows. But it remains a profound test of faith. Even more so when we hear these particular words of Jesus.

It does look as if Jesus was different. The Gospels present him as having his prayers answered almost all of the time and indeed he is sometimes his own answer to prayer. So he is not like us.

But I think there are three little clues in the passage that Jesus knew that his disciples would struggle with unanswered prayer. First, there is the very fact that he bothered to say these words. I suspect we are to hear them as encouragement rather than as guarantee – possibly. Second: they are linked to a rather left-field parable where God is compared to a grumpy neighbour who has already tucked himself and his family into bed but will nonetheless get up and help. The method is one of ludicrous comparison. Of course God is not like a grumpy neighbour! (Though there may be a hint here that persistence in prayer is part of the battle.) And thirdly, there is that little Lucan touch. What is the answer to prayer that is certainly promised? – it is the gift of God's Spirit. That may not in fact be what we have asked for, but it may be what we most need in order to cope with what is not answered.

37

Don't worry?

Luke 12:22-34

Surely this is Jesus at his most attractive: wise, calming, a sage. We may hear this in our culture as sounding like some modern Western hippy lifestyle but, in our over-working, over-consuming pressurised world, it sounds remarkably attractive. But what happens if we read it more carefully?

It could sound as if Jesus is offering a way to live which is dependent on a fatherly God who will provide for all our needs. But I wonder what this God will provide? It may be beautiful and nutritious but is it also likely to be simple and unglamorous – other-worldly? Because part of what is being taught is a letting go of the values of 'the world' with its false glamour. And there is dependence on God, but it is not so much a dependence that God will make everything tip-top in this world, as a confidence that if we give up wealth in this world – 'sell your possessions' – we will be rewarded in heaven. If we work for the Kingdom now, we will gain the Kingdom now and in the life to come, but without perhaps the trappings of monarchy!

I hope I am not making this sound too heavenly-minded to be of any earthly use, making it sound too unattractive. But the truth is that few Christians live like this, actually selling their possessions so they have money to give away to the poor because they trust in God's Kingdom now. The example, of course, that springs to mind is St Francis, first selling his father's possessions to feed the poor (but without his earthly father's permission!), and then stripping himself in public as a sign of giving up all his wealth so that he could follow Jesus literally. When I hear people talk of being fundamentalists or literalists or conservatives, I don't see them being fundamentalist or literalist or conservative about this text . . . But I think Jesus meant it. The truth is that it is too hard a teaching for most of us with families and homes and careers to follow literally. Even Francis' Franciscans found utter poverty too demanding. So perhaps we have to make do with relativising it – 'live simply that others may simply live' – but knowing we might not quite be getting the fierce radicality of Jesus' own commitment to the costly freedom of his God's Kingdom.

Do we like this God?

38

The parable of the prodigal son, or the ungracious elder brother, or the amazingly forgiving father
Luke 15:11-32

The more I read this parable, the more I think we have obscured its meaning and so its power by naming it 'The Parable of the Prodigal Son'. This character does take centre stage. This character is also the one that allows us preachers to cast our audiences as prodigal sons who need to repent and come home. But I wonder if that was Jesus' real point?

Who did he tell it to? We don't know exactly. Luke's Gospel contains some of the best-loved of Jesus' parables but sometimes included without much context, as here. But we can imagine it in a setting where Jesus is debating with proud religious people and trying to help them to see that the sinners he so loved – party animals, prostitutes, crooks – were welcome in God's Kingdom. And that they – the proud religious people – had got God wrong. We've already noticed what a constant theme in Jesus' life and teaching was subverting the self-confidence of the religiously powerful and right. Reminding them that they too are in need of the generous forgiveness of God and are not the gate-keepers to that forgiving love.

From that perspective, the most important character is in fact the self-righteous and disagreeable elder brother. And given the rather prissy and self-contained world of many of our modern churches, we may need to look at him hard.

But behind this both first- and twenty-first-century spiritual problem of the religious, there is a much deeper truth. The God who is longing for our return, watching and waiting for us. The shock of this parable was lost on me until I learned that Middle Eastern patriarchs didn't run and that important dignified people now don't run. (See K.E. Bailey's *Poet and Peasant* and *Through Peasant Eyes*.) But God runs to us. God does not stand on God's dignity when trying to reach humankind with love.

I think this is the heart of Luke's Gospel. We will hear deep echoes of it on the Cross. I think here Luke has taken us to Jesus' heart and the God he knew and embodied. This God touches my heart.

39

Zacchaeus

Luke 19:1-10

Let's meet another one of Jesus' unlikely friends, Zacchaeus. Zacchaeus is very rich. Of course he is very rich, he is a chief tax-collector and he has made his money taking a cut from the tax he has collected. This was common practice but no less resented for that. And it is likely that some of the tax he is collecting is going to the imperial administration. So he is a traitor as well. And worst of all, he is short. Probably has a bit of a 'Napoleon complex'. He is often portrayed as being without friends. No surprises there. I don't think I would have liked him!

But notice how Luke tells the story. Zacchaeus wants to see Jesus. We are not told why. Idle curiosity? Or a deeper need, even longing? Luke doesn't tell us. He doesn't need to. We can feel the character. This is great story-telling. No wonder the story was remembered.

And then Jesus looks up into the tree. Again, is this chance? It doesn't feel like it, but the point is not laboured. Jesus wants to eat with this man. THIS MAN. This unpleasant man. Sinner is too light a word to describe the contempt we ought to have for him. But Jesus wants to go into his home and taint himself by eating with him.

Of course he does. That's what Jesus does again and again. This is a lived example of the 'Parable of the Prodigal Son or . . .' He wants the despised and the outcast to know that God loves them.

The effect of course is delightfully revolutionary. Zacchaeus is melted and starts giving money away, as if he too believed in the Kingdom we read about earlier.

Notice that Jesus doesn't preach at Zacchaeus, but acceptance melts the hard heart. Jesus, I think we can be sure of this, longed for Zacchaeus to change but let love do the talking. Is this what it is like to come into the presence of God? To be so loved that hard sin is melted? Was that what it was like to meet God in Jesus?

40

The Triumphal Entry
Luke 19:29-44

I really want to focus on the second half of this passage but, for the sake of completeness (particularly as today is Palm Sunday for those reading through Lent), we must remember that Jesus' weeping over Jerusalem comes as he makes his 'triumphal entry'. It is an almost unbearably poignant moment. The crowds welcome Jesus as they have never quite welcomed him before. Surely this is the Messiah coming at last. It is his moment of greatest popularity. But as seems so frequent in human histories, it is also the moment when all is about to turn sour. But Jesus knows this.

One of the titles given to him was 'prophet'. Prophecy seems to be about seeing clearly what is happening now as well as seeing what may come. Jesus sees that this welcome is skin-deep because it is misguided. As in John's Gospel, when Jesus has to flee because the crowd want to make him king after he has fed them (John 6:15), so he knows that the real motive for the welcome now may be that people think he is coming as king to drive out the Romans. He will subvert this imminently by his assault on the Temple, but now he just weeps.

And he weeps because he can see that the mistaken choice of violence as opposed to grace will lead to violent repression. There has been discussion as to whether the language Jesus uses here is prophetic – he could see the future with the Romans destroying Jerusalem after the failed rebellion – or whether it is language that is shaped by the fact that Luke's Gospel was written after that terrible event. In fact, it is also possible that Jesus, being far-sighted, could simply see the inevitable consequence of the choices being made. Either way, he can imagine the horror of a siege and he weeps.

And he weeps because it is unnecessary. The Jerusalem religious authorities and the ordinary people had been offered a choice. In the light of what we have read in Luke so far, we might want to say that they had been offered a choice of working with God's love for everyone, including the hated oppressors, or not. And they had chosen not to heed this love. And the consequences were all too human and all too horrible.

These are my words, but notice how Jesus describes this, as a 'visitation from God'. Now this is entirely consistent with the prophetic writings – see Jeremiah or Hosea. But if we are asking ourselves whether Jesus is a window into the nature of God, what might this say about God's reaction to bad human choices?

41

Jesus cleanses the Temple
Luke 19:45-48

In Luke, Matthew and Mark, the Triumphal Entry leads straight to the cleansing of the Temple. Jesus goes straight for the heart of the religious establishment and attacks it for corruption. The sort of corruption that makes a profit out of people's religious needs and access to God. Behind this lies a deeper corruption: the corruption that assumes God is an object to be ignored or manipulated. Because knowledge of the real God would make selling access to God an abomination. The gracious real God would not make access dependent on money and ritual.

Luke tells the story succinctly and modestly. The other Gospel accounts include much more detail, much more violence and anger. Jesus is described as using a *phragellion*, a multi-stranded whip, and overturning the tables of the traders. Truly, zeal for God's house was burning within him.

Again, this may make us uncomfortable. 'Gentle Jesus, meek and mild' would not do this. Isn't anger always wrong?

The classic theological defence of this is that, whereas it might be wrong for us fallen sinners, the fact that Jesus was perfect means he can be angry and not commit sin.

I am not comfortable with this distinction. I recognise that some (much, most) of my anger may be self-deceiving, but I do not think that in principle human anger at injustice is self-deceiving. When wealthy pop stars get angry about starving children, I may feel queasy, but it is not wrong to be angry when the helpless are made to suffer. And anger motivates me. It releases energy in me. Is this bad? Not sustainable, of course. But good in short bursts, perhaps.

And Jesus is fully human, completely human, human like you and me. Of course he gets angry in good causes. He is violently angry here (though I still like to think that he did not hurt any individual . . .)

Again, let us ask ourselves one of our persistent questions: what might this tell us about God? Rightly, we have moved away from preaching an angry God whose first response is judgement: if for no other reason than that this image was used to try to frighten people into obedience and silence, including in the face of profound injustice. I suspect the Church is still reaping the harvest of this abuse. But does this mean that God is never angry?

We know that we should not anthropomorphise God. Just like Disney is not a great guide to the behaviour of real animals, so simply projecting our emotions on to God is an unreliable theological method. But the scriptures often portray a God angry at sin, especially injustice. I don't want to believe in a God who is indifferent to injustice. So perhaps Jesus is a good guide here too?

42

The parable of the wicked tenants
Luke 20:9-19

How did Jesus think about himself? What was going on inside his head? This is a hugely difficult question. We do not have simple and direct access to Jesus' self-consciousness. The language of sonship was close to his heart. Perhaps this parable may take us under his skin.

It is a classic parable of Jesus. We find it elsewhere (Matthew 21:33-46; Mark 12:1-12) and we find other parables with this style and shape. Its purpose was clear. It was to link Jesus to the long line of prophets who had come before him with God's message but been rejected. So that when he too would be rejected, as he was already being rejected by the religious authorities, people would understand that this was part of a long pattern of hard-hearted resistance to God. Jesus was claiming this authority for himself.

But he went further. He played the part of the most important messenger, the son. No more important representative could be sent than a son. A son embodied the authority, the very presence, of the father. The wicked tenants in the story got this. To kill the son was to destroy the authority of the father, for the father and the son were as one. So they kill him.

When we add this parable to the many examples of Jesus addressing God as his father, I think we have been given an insight into how Jesus saw himself, as being in a son-relationship to God as father. This is not simply to import back into the Gospels the later theological formulae of the Church, but this does enable us to see where they come from, and that they are not as far-fetched as some of the recent critics of the Church have alleged.

I am sure that, in Jesus' head and heart, he conceived of himself as being in a son-like relationship to God. This was in part an inclusive spiritual insight – so he encouraged others to pray to God as father – but it was also distinctive, in that he had a particular role as 'son' to fulfil. And central to that particular role, by this stage in Jesus' life and ministry, is a conviction that he must be rejected and die sacrificially to save his people. It is the peculiar responsibility of the son. We must look on and wonder.

43
The coming of the 'Son of Man'
Luke 21:34-38

Frankly, I would rather not be writing this reflection. The history of Christian Apocalyptic (I mean, by this shorthand, Christian imagining of the end of the world) is not always impressive. Yes, it has had the huge positive of giving Christians courage when living in oppressive regimes and also of subverting the glamour of the world now, but it has also contributed to deceptive fantasies, some of which have been cruel and arrogant, some of which have helped Christians to opt out of working for God's Kingdom now.

But it would be dishonest to pretend that this is not an important strand of the New Testament, including for Jesus. He used this elusive little phrase, the 'Son of Man', to describe himself, which has its roots partly in the apocalyptic sections of the Book of Daniel. The 'Son of Man' is both a human figure and a figure from the divine court. And in today's passage, Jesus is using it to describe himself coming again as judge. I could have chosen a number of such passages, but have chosen this as one example.

Is Jesus just going mad? Has the stress of the conflict with the religious authorities, and the intensity of his own conviction that the only way to save his people is to die for them, driven him over the edge? Is this a 'make believe' that, even if he dies, he will come back, justified, with full authority? I ask these blunt, even disrespectful, questions, because Jesus' language here (however much it is stylised like much apocalyptic, as well as refined by Luke) is strange. 'The day' will come and it will come 'upon the whole earth'. It will be a day of judgement. The people are to pray that they will be able to 'stand' – i.e. stand and be justified as in a court – before the Son of Man.

I don't think Jesus is going mad here. In a few days' time, we will have to begin thinking about the Resurrection and, however challenging that is, and however strange it is that Jesus is presented in the Gospels as often hinting at a coming resurrection and at his 'coming again' while nevertheless suffering agonies of doubt in the Garden of Gethsemane and on the Cross, I think that the frequency of these references indicates that this was part of Jesus' later beliefs and that the Gospels are faithfully recording them.

I find myself having to do a lot of 'translation' in my head before I can relate to this language. I cannot imagine how a Second Coming would occur. Would Jesus – looking like what? – arrive on a mountain top in Israel, as some claim to believe? What would the TV cameras see? What about the people who would be asleep on the far side of the planet? How long would the trials take? And so on. If I try to get too literalistic about a Second Coming, I end up sounding silly.

But spiritually, belief in a Second Coming is, ironically, helpful. It does keep me, at least a little bit, more up to the mark to imagine Jesus coming back today. What am I doing today? Is it a good use of the gift of time and energy and resources? How would it feel if Jesus came back, right this very second? Would I be comfortable if 'He' saw me doing this? It is a way – carefully handled – of building accountability into daily living.

Further, the Second Coming reminds us that, ultimately, God is in control. It may or may not be helpful to imagine Jesus arriving on a mountain top in Israel. It is certainly helpful to remember that, in the chaos of this world, God is sovereign and 'all shall be well'.

I hope you may find these translation strategies helpful as you wrestle with these baffling texts.

But whether Jesus was right or mad depends, of course, on our view of the Resurrection.

44

The Last Supper
Luke 22:14-27

If you are reading this in Lent, today is Maundy Thursday. As a priest, it is the most moving day on which to lead a celebration of the Eucharist: Lord's Supper, Holy Communion, Mass – as far as this is concerned, they all feel the same. It is the day on which I have the closest imaginative connection to Jesus. I can feel him breaking the bread and sharing the wine, and the heartbreak of it. He knew the end was coming and he wanted his disciples to be able to endure and indeed build long into the future. He wants them to remember him, to re-encounter him as they do this again in the future, and to keep his values.

Sacred meals are not uncommon in religions. But this is a profoundly uncomfortable one. For Jesus, taking the very ordinary stuff of a meal, bread and wine, and using it to remind his friends of his body and blood, is brutal. As a professional priest, I do it so often that the shock of it is normally lost on me, until I am preparing children to receive Communion for the first time, and they go 'eergh'. It is too visceral to use white bread to remind us of the white flesh of a body and red wine to remind us of red blood.

I know it is a symbol, but feel the strangeness with me. How did that morsel of bread feel in the mouths of the disciples? Did it clag in their mouths? Did they gag as they swallowed the wine? Why was Jesus so brutally down to earth?

I don't know. I do know that there is something solid about meeting him in a piece of bread chewed, and in a sip of wine swallowed. When life is tumultuous and my brain scrambled, and God feels unwordable, this is solidity on which I can rest. And when life feels too horrible, then as I break the bread and pour the wine, knowing that he too was broken and poured out, somehow that brings God healingly into the mess. Was this his intention? I don't know. But it works for me and I am grateful.

I am also worried. Because Luke goes on to remind us, by placing these words of Jesus here, that even after this most sacred of moments disciples can behave appallingly – arrogant, indifferent, cruel. Me too, and many other Christians down the ages. Perhaps we need the brutality of the bread/body and the wine/blood to remind us of the cost of our sin and prevent us from falling or draw us back when we have fallen?

45

The Crucifixion
Luke 23:32-43

This feels like the heart of Luke's Gospel. Notice that the way he tells the story is different from Mark and Matthew. It is Luke who gives us the words of forgiveness from the Cross. It is Luke who gives us the dialogue with the dying criminal. Whether Luke had different sources or told the story differently is not a question for now. But I do want to stress that we need to hear what Luke is saying here because it is so distinctive.

Luke is telling us that Jesus forgives. Again and again in his Gospel, we have seen Jesus forgive even the most wicked of sinners. Indeed, long before they have repented, Jesus wants to spend time with them. He was clearly longing for them to find freedom and new life. And he seems to let them back in on the basis of such little evidence of change, or sanctification as we used to say. Think of the Prodigal Son – and there is clearly a link in Luke between that parable and what happens on the Cross. He has made a move but he has barely had a chance to open his mouth before the Forgiving Father is throwing his arms around him and welcoming him home. So too here: the criminal dying on the cross next to Jesus only has the insight and the energy to speak two sentences. But on the basis of this, Jesus promises him life in Paradise. This man who has certainly lived a bad life – thieving, probably murdering – has signed no statement of faith, has not been baptised, has not received the right hand of fellowship, has not given a lifetime of service to God, does not know any creed, but just sees something in Jesus and trusts him. It is enough.

This could feel very unfair. This criminal just slips in at the last minute, despite my lifetime of service. But think again of the parable of the Grumpy Elder Brother. Jesus does not think that God keeps a simplistic count of goodness. Have you done enough to get into Paradise? It is not like that. It is fundamentally mercy, grace. (If you want to think of it technically, this is a pure example of that old Reformation doctrine of 'justification by faith'.) But actually I don't feel this is unfair. I am, rather, deeply touched that Jesus shows such loving mercy when he himself is in such a terrible place. I am glad he is like this. This is why I follow him.

And Jesus clearly thought this was what God is like: the forgiving Father who is waiting, poised, to welcome us home. And if I am drawn to Jesus, perhaps I too can be drawn to put my faith in this God in whom Jesus believed, and who may be the best window into God we have been given.

And on Good Friday might we ask ourselves: if God is really like this, how might I live and how should our Church be?

46

Burial

Luke 23:50-56

If you are reading this in Lent, today in the Church's calendar is called Holy Saturday. It is the profoundest day of waiting in the Church's year.

It is over. Jesus is dead. Truly dead. His spirit gone out of his body. Rigor mortis will be setting in. Often a dead body immediately after death does not look attractive. The blood seems to go from the skin and it becomes yellow and translucent. The muscles seem to sink so the body looks more skeletal. It goes cold quite quickly. This is what Jesus looked like. Really dead and then really buried. As his disciples, we must not in any way pretend that he did not die.

And then we wait. Every year on this day I find myself wondering, 'Will I believe in the Resurrection in the morning?' 'Will I feel it again this year?' And the truth is that every year I don't know. I must just wait. We have to do a lot of waiting in life. Sometimes it is just a queue! But sometimes we are waiting for news of a medical test. Sometimes we are sitting by a bedside as someone is dying. Sometimes, we are looking at a terrible mess in the world or Church and asking, 'How much longer, God?' And we want God to answer. We want God to hurry.

We want God to give us an assurance now that good news is coming. And God does not. We have to wait.

Why did God wait three days to raise Jesus? Why not have him rise from the foot of the Cross? Or on the Saturday morning? I don't know and we are not told, so guessing is a bit pointless. But the consequence was real waiting.

It was, however, waiting in prayer. The Sabbath was a day when ordinary activity was put aside so people could focus on God. If they are like us, probably not consciously all the time. Their minds wandered like ours do! But God had built a structure into their life which was about stopping. So Jesus' disciples have to stop and wait.

God's timing really is not our timing. I am not patient, but I understand that I need to learn to wait on God in prayer. Thank God for Holy Saturday.

47

Resurrection
Luke 24:1-12

The Gospels were written backwards. By which I mean that they were written because people believed that Jesus had been raised from the dead. It is possible that people would have preserved some of Jesus' sayings, because of their wisdom and beauty, but they would not have bothered to tell his life story if they did not believe that he was still alive. And had been raised to life by God, thereby justifying his teaching and actions. So Luke 24 is the beginning of his Gospel.

It is important to stress this simple reality because in our country there is still a mood around that 'Jesus was a good man but how can he be God's Son?' I understand that difficulty. Jesus was a good man and it is not easy to put into words how a truly human being can also be God present amongst us. But the truth is, our knowledge of Jesus is based on this indescribable reality, that a human body, which was truly dead, was really resurrected. Now the resurrected body was not the same as the body that died. All of the Gospels show that. It was deeply mysterious. But it was still Jesus. God had miraculously, supernaturally, amazingly, resurrected him – even if the Gospels are delightfully vague about what actually happened and how. The first disciples didn't understand. They were amazed and frightened. Perhaps we might learn something from them and not domesticate Easter Sunday?

In other words, Jesus is about God from beginning to end. We asked ourselves a question at the beginning of this book: can we see through Jesus to God? I think the Resurrection says, 'Of course you can'. God gives us Jesus so that we can see God more clearly. And I like what I see. It is not always easy to understand, but I like this God who is not churchy, who is relaxed about rules, who likes dodgy people, who loves people whom the elite and religious don't like, who throws his arms around those who take even the slightest of steps towards him. And we see all this in a real flesh-and-blood human being who is also one of us. So that we can understand, even if just a little, and we can believe: 'we could be like this too'.

So do please spend some time looking at Jesus, looking at Jesus and through Jesus to God, and rejoice: 'God loves you like Jesus does'. And then ask for help to live the way Jesus lived, as another of God's children.

Bibliography

Longer academic Bible commentaries

- J.B. Green, *The Gospel of Luke* (Grand Rapids and Cambridge: Eerdmans, 1997).

- L.T. Johnson, *The Gospel of Luke* (Collegeville, Minnesota: Liturgical Press, 1991).

- I. Howard Marshall, *The Gospel of Luke. A Commentary on the Greek Text* (Exeter: Paternoster, 1978).

- J. Nolland, *Luke* (Nashville/Dallas: Word, 1989 & 1993, 3 vols.).

For historic readings see:

- A.A. Just (ed.), *Ancient Christian Commentary on Scripture. New Testament III. Luke* (Downers Grove, Illinois: IVP, 2003).

- B. Kreitzer (ed.), *Reformation Commentary on Scripture. New Testament III. Luke* (Downers Grove, Illinois: IVP Academic, 2015).

Shorter more accessible Bible commentaries

- R.T. France, *Luke* (Grand Rapids, Michigan: Baker, 2013).

- Tom Wright, *Luke for Everyone* (London: SPCK, 2001).

Books reflecting on Luke

- K.E. Bailey, *Poet and Peasant* and *Through Peasant Eyes* (Grand Rapids, Michigan: Eerdmans, 1976).

- I. Howard Marshall, *Luke – historian and theologian* (Exeter: Paternoster, 1970).

- F. Scott Spencer, *Salty wives, spirited mothers and savvy widows. Capable women of purpose and persistence in Luke's Gospel* (Grand Rapids, Michigan, and Cambridge: Eerdmans, 2012).